D0720587

AN IDEAS INTO ACTION GUIDEBOOK

Leadership Networking

Connect, Collaborate, Create

IDEAS INTO ACTION GUIDEBOOKS

Aimed at managers and executives who are concerned with their own and others' development, each guidebook in this series gives specific advice on how to complete a developmental task or solve a leadership problem.

LEAD CONTRIBUTORS	Curt Grayson
	David Baldwin
CONTRIBUTORS	Kate Beatty
	Gene Klann
	Cynthia D. McCauley
	Eric Roth
	Cresencio Torres
DIRECTOR OF PUBLICATIONS	Martin Wilcox
EDITOR	Peter Scisco
ASSOCIATE EDITOR	Karen Mayworth
WRITER	Rebecca Garau
DESIGN AND LAYOUT	Joanne Ferguson
CONTRIBUTING ARTISTS	Laura J. Gibson
	Chris Wilson, 29 & Company

CCL No. 433
ISBN No. 978-1-882197-97-2

CENTER FOR CREATIVE LEADERSHIP
WWW.CCL.ORG

AN IDEAS INTO ACTION GUIDEBOOK

Leadership Networking

Connect, Collaborate, Create

Curt Grayson and David Baldwin

Center for
Creative
Leadership®

THE IDEAS INTO ACTION GUIDEBOOK SERIES

This series of guidebooks draws on the practical knowledge that the Center for Creative Leadership (CCL®) has generated, since its inception in 1970, through its research and educational activity conducted in partnership with hundreds of thousands of managers and executives. Much of this knowledge is shared—in a way that is distinct from the typical university department, professional association, or consultancy. CCL is not simply a collection of individual experts, although the individual credentials of its staff are impressive; rather it is a community, with its members holding certain principles in common and working together to understand and generate practical responses to today's leadership and organizational challenges.

The purpose of the series is to provide managers with specific advice on how to complete a developmental task or solve a leadership challenge. In doing that, the series carries out CCL's mission to advance the understanding, practice, and development of leadership for the benefit of society worldwide. We think you will find the Ideas Into Action Guidebooks an important addition to your leadership toolkit.

Table of Contents

EXECUTIVE BRIEF

Networking is essential to effective leadership in today's organizations. Leaders who are skilled networkers have access to
people, information, and resources to help solve problems and
create opportunities. Leaders who neglect their networks are
missing out on a critical component of their role as leaders. This
book will help leaders take a new view of networking and provide insight into how to enhance their networks and become
effective at leadership networking.

Networking for Leaders

Welcome to the network! Were you aware that you're already a member? A network is a set of connected relationships with people inside and outside your organization upon whom you depend to accomplish your work. Within your existing network, you share information, collaborate, and solve problems. Sometimes you pitch in or cover for each other, make referrals, endorse and support. Other times you push back or offer criticism. Within your network, there are differences of opinion, even cliques and conflict. From your current position, you influence and respond to the network.

Conventional wisdom often places networking in the context of looking for a new job, chatting at parties and events, or working in sales. The ability to network is useful in those situations, but it is in the day-to-day work of leading where networking becomes an essential and indispensable skill. Leadership networking is not about collecting business cards or schmoozing. Leadership networking is about building relationships and making alliances in service of others—customers, clients, constituents, peers, bosses, and employees—and in service of the organization's work and goals. A robust leadership network helps provide access to people, information, and resources. Leaders can use those connections to solve problems and create opportunities.

Intentionally developing, maintaining, and using contacts and alliances are at the heart of leadership networking. Managers who develop their skill at these tasks build relationships throughout the organization and expand their pool of resources to include people and organizations on the outside: customers, clients, vendors, media, industry experts, and so on. Over time, these leaders create broad-based and strong networks that provide greater

7

access to the information and resources they need to reach their goals. Through their networks, they

- increase effectiveness by deepening and broadening the communication channels between individuals and groups

- remove political roadblocks by bridging distances that separate positions, work groups, teams, and business units

- open up new opportunities and uncover ideas by "cross-pollinating" with other groups and individuals who may connect in ways not readily apparent

- strengthen their power base by delivering support and resources to groups and individuals in need, by accepting resources as required, and by broadcasting the availability of talent and resources found in their group

- gain exposure across their organizations by highlighting individual efforts and the work of their groups in achieving organizational goals

Still, many managers in leadership roles are ambivalent about or even averse to the idea of networking. They have seen colleagues aggressively network for personal gain. They may view networking as an uncomfortable or tedious process. Some managers consider themselves too busy to give attention to networking, and even if they see its value, they think the organization should value their individual contributions even more. But becoming a more effective leader requires not only developing their skills and capabilities as individuals, but also developing relationships with others. If managers who struggle with either the concept or the practice of networking can set aside their preconceived notions, they can develop skills that take networking to a different level.

Beyond Conventional Wisdom

Aspects of conventional networking are useful, but for long-term or complex situations a leadership view of networking is essential.

Conventional networking can be seen as . . .	Leadership networking should be . . .
transaction based	relationship based
one way	two way
investing in self first	investing in others first
providing contacts	providing resources to get work done
a source of information	a forum for sharing and problem solving
expanding address book	building alliances
building number of contacts	leading to greater access and influence
short term	long term
limited	in depth
individual	organizational

 Reflections on Networking

What benefits have you experienced with networking? How has networking helped you professionally? Are there situations where networking helped you accomplish your work?

_____

_____

_____

9

Mapping Your Network

In traditional organizations, managers accomplish their work through others in a direct reporting structure.

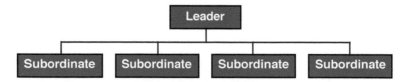

Although this structure still exists in some organizations, in many others the traditional hierarchy has changed significantly. In many cases, this is because new technologies make it easier to share information and connect with others. Regardless of how an organization might draw its formal structure, the arrangement of the work itself looks more like a web and less like a pyramid.

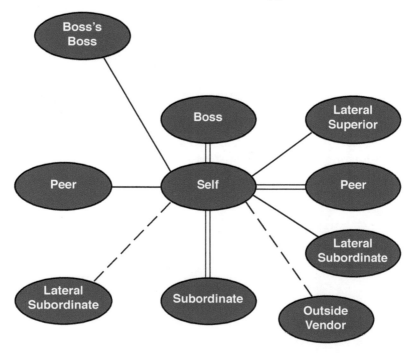

In this fluid, multidimensional environment, leaders are more dependent upon other people to get access, information, and resources to accomplish tasks and goals. They get things done through a large and often diverse network of people over whom they have little (if any) direct control. Much of their work is accomplished by using relationship-rich skills like influence, communication, and political savvy. Leadership networking provides a conduit and a context for using those kinds of skills to get results.

Six Requirements of Leadership Networking

Improving your leadership network takes time, and it begins with assessing your current network, its strengths, and its weaknesses. It also takes your personal commitment to act in ways that strengthen the relationships in your network and cultivate the relationships you need in your network. Later in this guidebook, we offer specific strategies for developing your leadership network. But first, let's take a look at six critical requirements of leadership networking.

1 **Leadership Networking Demands Authenticity**
You will be most effective in building your leadership network if you maintain a genuine objective of building relationships, providing support, and accomplishing the work for the benefit of the organization. Your authenticity will generate trust in others; people are drawn to leaders who are sincere and genuine. Networking is not a ploy for getting your way. People will see through attempts at networking that are self-serving or manipulative. If you earn a reputation as someone who takes but doesn't give, who

11

What Does Your Network Look Like?

Using the organizational diagram at the bottom of page 10 as a model, map your own current leadership network. This type of diagram is a visual picture of the people you interact with to accomplish your work. Having a picture of your network in mind is the first step toward developing or improving your leadership networking skills.

In the space provided on the next page, add ovals with the names of those with whom you have important work relationships (your boss, direct reports, peers, boss's boss, customers, vendors, and so on). Draw double lines to people with whom you interact frequently, draw single lines to people with whom you interact less frequently, and draw dotted lines to people with whom you rarely interact.

Modify this activity so that it's an accurate reflection of your network. For example, if you work in sales or purchasing, your relationships with clients or vendors may be your most important relationships—even more important that your relationship with your boss.

After you complete your diagram, answer the following questions:

Is your network larger or smaller than you would have expected?

_____

How much do you depend upon your direct reports?

_____

How much do you depend upon people who are outside your scope of authority? _____

_____

Given that you've identified all of these as important work relationships, what determines how much you interact with different people? _____

_____

Network Diagram

Self

uses information inappropriately, or who breaks confidences, your networks will shut down. Regaining the trust and respect needed to rebuild will not be easy—if possible at all.

2 **Leadership Networking Trades in Resources**

Having resources such as information, services, access, and power that can be contributed to organizational projects builds a leadership network through give-and-take. Reciprocity is important in creating, keeping, and using your leadership network. Leaders who are skilled at this kind of bartering know their assets and share them appropriately. For example, a manager may assign an individual with excellent presentation skills to a team that seeks visibility with top executives, routinely give a peer a preview of monthly sales reports, or offer personal time to advocate for another's cause. Consider how each of you contributes to the overall organization's goals, and how working together might make both of you more effective toward that end.

3 **Leadership Networking Calls for Thoughtful and Deliberate Use of Power**

Within an organization, a good definition of *power* is the ability to get things done. Some power comes from your position, such as the ability to reward and punish. But that kind of power is impossible to use effectively in most network relationships. In the context of leadership networking, there are three sources of power. Regardless of the source of your power, it's important to use it wisely, in a way that maintains your authenticity and the trust others have in you.

Reputation. Who you are, how you lead, and what you have accomplished determine your reputation in an organization.

14

People are naturally drawn to leaders who are competent and successful, and they're naturally hesitant to network with those who have a bad attitude, who don't have a strong work ethic, and who are marginal performers. If you are known as someone who gets results and who can be held accountable, you gain power from your positive reputation.

Alliances. The quality of your network affects others. If you have connections to other key influencers and decision makers, your perceived power increases.

Position. The nature of your work generates power. If you are involved in the organization's greatest priorities or problems, your visibility and role add to your power.

4 **Leadership Networking Requires Skillful Communication**
Much of the effectiveness of a leadership network depends on whether you can communicate in a way that builds awareness of your needs and your assets. If you cannot make others aware of what you can bring to bear on a problem or project and what you need in order to accomplish goals of your own, your networking strategies will be largely ineffectual. Creating that awareness means disseminating information accurately, timely, and clearly. It requires that you have the listening skills necessary to elicit and absorb information from others. And it demands that you know when to speak and when to listen. Consider a manager with excellent speaking skills, who can clearly communicate a point of view or share information. If that same manager can't hear and understand the perspectives and needs of others, the relationships in his or her leadership network are weakened because the communication channel works in only one direction.

15

5 **Leadership Networking Calls for Savvy Negotiating Skill**
Effective negotiators know when to push hard and when to back off, when to share information and when to hold back, when to swap resources, and when to trade short-term outcomes for a long-term goal. This skill is linked closely to being aware of resources and needs—those that you have and those that others have. A manager who is known to always play hardball or a manager who is viewed as a pushover has very little room to negotiate within a network.

6 **Leadership Networking Means Managing Conflict**
The definition of *network* implies that conflicts within networks usually cannot be resolved in a win-lose way. Very seldom do you have enough power over peers, lateral subordinates, superiors, and external contacts to force them to act in ways that are not in their self-interest. You need skills for resolving conflict with win-win or win-learn solutions. When conflict occurs within your network, work to appreciate the opposing point of view. Look for points of mutual agreement. Express your position in a way that is helpful to resolving the conflict by drawing on your influence skills.

Barriers to Building a Leadership Network

The nature of networking—working with and through others over whom you have no direct control—means that building and using networks can be difficult, even problematic. Identifying the people and groups with whom you should connect is often the easiest part. However, in the process of building and maintaining relationships, leaders are likely to face a number of barriers. Any one

16

barrier can pose a challenge to effective networking; often a number of factors conspire to prevent good networks from developing.

Operational Differences

Valuable networking relationships may be thwarted because of the operations of the organization. Working in different functions, departments, or divisions can make networking seem too unnatural or out of the way. Different bosses, goals, and objectives may set up competitive—even adversarial—relationships, rather than collaborative ones.

Level Differences

The structure of the organization can make building and maintaining important network relationships harder. When leaders try to network with someone higher or lower on the organizational chart, issues of power, access, and agendas can get in the way. For example, it is often your boss's boss who is critical

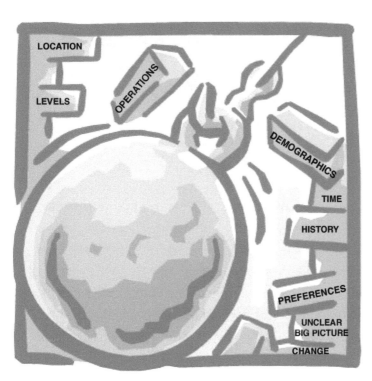

in defining your agenda and providing the resources you need, yet he or she is not always accessible. The stronger the hierarchy of an organization and the more people believe in following the chain of command, the more difficult this level difference becomes.

Demographic Differences

People more readily and easily make connections with people they view as similar to themselves. As a result, networking with others who differ from you by race, gender, age, country of origin, and socioeconomic status may require greater effort. A leader who is in a demographic minority in the organization may have to overcome a sense of isolation in order to network. Conversely, a leader who is in the demographic mainstream must not mistake familiar networks for effective networks.

Desirable Diversity

It's important for your network to bridge diverse groups of people. If everyone in your network already interacts with each other, the network won't be as useful as it otherwise could be. Building a network of people who do not regularly interact gives you the opportunity to tap into more diverse subgroups.

Personal Preferences

Personality and patterns of behavior can make the process of effective networking more or less challenging. Leaders who are outgoing or collaborative usually network more readily than leaders who tend to be reserved or independent. Networking will be more of a stretch for someone who is more introverted than for someone who is extroverted and thrives on interaction with colleagues. This is not to say you must try to change your personality or how you are hardwired if you fall into the more introverted camp in order to be an effective leadership networker. It simply means you will have to go against the grain somewhat to find, maintain, and effectively utilize your network.

Other Barriers

Effective networking can also be blocked by other factors.

Unclear big picture. One possible barrier to effective networking is a lack of understanding of your own role in helping your organization succeed, as well as a lack of understanding of others' roles in achieving that same end. Without an understanding of the big picture that your organization is working toward, it is hard to connect to each other.

Time. Already pressed for time, leaders may see the investment in networking as too consuming.

Location. Working with colleagues in other locations—often in different countries or time zones—can become a barrier to building effective two-way relationships. Even seemingly innocuous circumstances, such as working on a different floor or in a

---

Thinking Globally

Building a network across national boundaries can be difficult, but very worthwhile. Perhaps you can't just walk down the hall to talk to your intended network partner, but networking is still possible through technology and travel. You're likely to face significant differences—in culture, language, religion, values, education, political systems, socioeconomic factors, and family and socialization practices. The greater those differences, the harder it may be to build the trust on which a good network is based. Leaders who seek to understand different cultures and the most effective ways to network will succeed. And given that diversity in a network is a good thing, having the opportunity to build a global network is a great advantage. It gives your network the potential to be much richer and more diverse.

---

different building, can contribute to making interactions, and therefore relationships, more difficult.

Previous relationship history. A positive experience or relationship is a boost to building effective networks. On the other hand, a negative experience or perception can be incredibly difficult to overcome.

Change. Organizational restructuring, new management, and changing roles can throw a wrench into well-functioning networks and relationships. Organizational changes may change the organization's goals—and individuals' roles in meeting those goals.

Assessing Your Network

This section serves as a workbook to help you understand your leadership network, identify your most important relationships, and diagnose weaknesses and gaps. It includes four brief activities, along with questions for reflection, to help you clarify your situation prior to setting networking goals.

1. Think about your current priorities or leadership challenges. Perhaps you are a leader of a team responsible for a new product launch that is behind schedule. Perhaps you're working to implement a new training program. Or maybe you're struggling to manage a difficult employee. Whatever your key challenge is, take a moment and write it down:

_____

_____

_____

2. Next, create a network diagram directly related to your leadership challenge. Who could help you meet this challenge? Indicate how often you interact with double lines (frequently), single lines (less frequently), and dotted lines (rarely). If you don't know of a specific person, write a position, department, or function. (One of your networking tasks would then be to find out names you need to add to your network.)

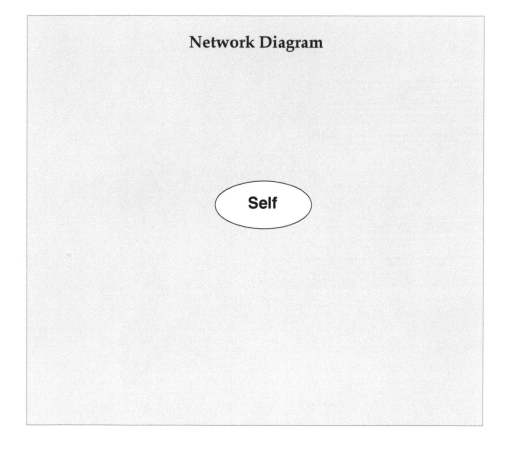

3. Look at the people you included on your diagram. How important is each person in terms of your ability to face or resolve your leadership challenge? Label each name in the diagram with a 1 (very important), 2 (moderately important), or 3 (not very important).

4. Write the name of each person you ranked as very important at the top of a column. Then rate the effectiveness of your relationship with each person by responding to the statements at the left. Use the following scale:

| 1 never | 2 rarely | 3 sometimes | 4 often | 5 always |

I understand this person's goals and needs.					
I have access to information from this person.					
I share information with this person.					
I am comfortable asking for resources from this person.					
I offer my resources to this person.					
I trust this person.					
I frankly discuss concerns or problems with this person.					
I can influence this person.					
I am open to this person's influence.					

If you rated your very important relationships at 4 or 5, this indicates solid networking relationships. You can depend on these people and they can depend on you—an ideal situation. If you rated your key relationships as less effective (meaning that you gave them ratings of mostly 1 and 2), then you are in a situation of depending on people without being able to count on their support. If your responses for a person are scattered across 1 through 5, your relationship with that person is inconsistent, but you have a foundation on which you can develop an effective relationship.

5. After completing the four activities above, reflect on the following questions.

- Are your relationships helping or hurting you when it comes to meeting your leadership challenge?

- What experiences or behaviors have contributed to your stronger relationships?

- What experiences or behaviors have contributed to your weaker relationships?

- What makes you a valuable component of other people's networks?

- What do you share or contribute most often?

- What do you seek or require most often?

- How can you utilize your strong network relationships in service of your leadership challenge?

- What are some ways you could begin to strengthen the weaker relationships in service of your leadership challenge?

- What do your less effective relationships have in common? What patterns do you see in how you interact in these relationships?

- Looking at your networking difficulties, what have you learned?

23

Identifying and Analyzing Barriers

Review your analysis of how effective your network relationships are. For those relationships that you rated as less effective, what are the possible causes? Are operational differences, level differences, demographic differences, personal preferences, or some other kind of barriers standing in the way?

Use this worksheet to analyze and record what is keeping specific relationships from being as effective as they could be. Use the following code:

OD—operational differences, LD—level differences, DD—demographic differences, PP—personal preferences, O—other

Person	Barrier	Your Analysis of the Barrier
Will Smithson	OD	His office is in another building, and his department has different pressures.
Martha Pritchett	LD	She is a lateral superior. I need her buy-in more than she needs my services.

24

Strategies for Developing Your Leadership Network

A strong and vibrant leadership network requires time and effort. But the work and understanding involved don't have to overwhelm you. Once you understand how your present network is structured, who is involved, and where you can push your network to the next level, you can take action using these eight strategies.

Learn from Others

Individuals who learn by accessing others seek advice, examples, support, or instruction from people who have met a challenge similar to the one they face, or they learn how to do something by watching someone else do it. Who networks well in your organization or in your community? What exactly do they do, and what do they say? Try similar tactics or approaches. Ask them to talk to you about their view of networking and how they build and use relationships.

> Keep a networking notebook for a week. Observe people around you in meetings, working together, and in casual interactions. Who seems connected? Who seems isolated? What specifically are they doing? What clues does this activity give you as to how you should act and how you should treat others?

Invite Others

Bring others into your world. Invite them to lunch. Find time for a fifteen- or thirty-minute conversation to find out what is happening in their world and to tell them what you and your group are doing. Invite others to your meetings and ask them to contribute their expertise and their perspective, or to explore possible connections between their work and yours.

25

> Arrange one invitation each week. One week you may ask a teammate to talk for fifteen minutes after a meeting and ask for an opinion on another project. The next week, you could invite a peer to lunch. Keep up the once-a-week practice, and soon it will be routine.

Invite Yourself

Ask to sit in on another group's meeting or planning session. Join a committee or group outside your own area.

> Set a goal to join a new committee or task force in the next month. If you don't know what options you have, spend a week gathering ideas. Talk to your boss, ask a peer, or check in with human resources.

Ask for Feedback

Seek honest answers from peers, direct reports, and superiors to gain a clear picture of how you and your group function and what impact you have on others. Feedback engages others in a constructive way by adding depth to existing relationships.

> Seek feedback on a regular basis, after you have set goals for developing your leadership network. Ask for specific comments about how others see you in regard to your relationships with others, how you share information, how you use your influence, and other networking skills.

Work with Others

Volunteer for assignments or projects that give you an opportunity to work across functions. One of the best ways to build connections with others is to work together on something. A fringe benefit is the visibility you will gain with people outside your department.

> Volunteer for the next assignment that involves people outside your work group. Whatever it is—a presentation to senior management, giving a plant tour, working on a cross-functional team—raise your hand and take that step forward.

Be Direct

Let people know what you are doing, why it matters, and how it relates to their work or goals. By communicating clearly, you help others see how they can connect to you and your work to achieve their own goals.

> Talk to your direct reports about leadership networking. Tell them you are making efforts to extend your network and that you want their input. Ask them about their projects and challenges. Make a list of people, departments, or functions that could be helpful in accomplishing their goals—seek and incorporate information from your direct reports in that list. With their help and input, make a plan that you and your direct reports can follow to create or improve your networks.

Be an Information Hub

Develop and offer yourself as a source of information about people, processes, and facts. Develop your ability to connect with strategic information about your organization.

> Make a list of your information assets. What do you know? What information does your group hold? How might your information be useful to others? Make a plan to disseminate information appropriately and intentionally.

Make Allies

You may be able to develop your networking skills by working with a mentor, colleague, or coach. For a source of coaching or mentoring, look to others you see as successful leadership networkers.

Interview effective networkers in your organization. Capture their specific behaviors. Ask them to observe your behaviors related to networking and to offer you feedback. You could also recruit a networking ally. The two of you could practice networking and give each other feedback, support, and encouragement.

Setting Goals and Taking Action

What can and what will you do to build and improve important work relationships? Using the eight ideas described in the previous section, think about what you can do differently to be more effective at leadership networking.

Many of the roles and skills expected and required of leaders today are connected to networking. If you aren't currently using your network to the fullest extent, you're missing out on benefits that can support your efforts to manage projects and lead people toward common goals. To build, maintain, and use your networks, you need to invest yourself in the process. You can't rely on other people to bring you into their networks.

Leadership networks require time and effort to develop. Using them to your advantage often requires that you break out of your routine and leave behind your usual way of doing things. If you are a talented individual contributor, for example, you may

Making Your Plan

Identify network relationships that you know you should develop and improve to accomplish your work. Then, as specifically as you can, write out actions you will take to improve them.

Person	Specific Action	Networking Benefit
Bill Jones (marketing)	I will set up a meeting.	Increased access to marketing data will help my team sell more products.
Christa Liu (head of sales for western division)	I will schedule a lunch to discuss areas of collaboration.	We will develop a better understanding of each other's team's needs.

need to learn how to more fully trust the talent and contributions of peers, direct reports, and superiors so that you can work collaboratively to reach goals you can't reach by yourself or in your own work group. By seeing networking as an integral part of your role as a leader and by taking action to develop and nurture related skills, you begin to create benefits for yourself, your group, and your organization.

29

Suggested Readings

Baldwin, D., & Grayson, C. (2004). *Influence: Gaining commitment, getting results.* Greensboro, NC: Center for Creative Leadership.

Cartwright, T. (2003). *Managing conflict with peers.* Greensboro, NC: Center for Creative Leadership.

Dalton, M. A. (1998). *Becoming a more versatile learner.* Greensboro, NC: Center for Creative Leadership.

Deal, J. J. (2007). *Retiring the generation gap: How employees young and old can find common ground.* San Francisco: Jossey-Bass.

Kaplan, R. E., & Mazique, M. (1983). *Trade routes: The manager's network of relationships.* Greensboro, NC: Center for Creative Leadership.

Kirkland, K., & Manoogian, S. (1998). *Ongoing feedback: How to get it, how to use it.* Greensboro, NC: Center for Creative Leadership.

Runde, C. E., & Flanagan, T. A. (2007). *Becoming a conflict competent leader: How you and your organization can manage conflict effectively.* San Francisco: Jossey-Bass.

Uzzi, B., & Dunlap, S. (2005). How to build your network. *Harvard Business Review, 83*(12), 53–60.

Background

Many participants in CCL's educational programs ask for advice on how to network more effectively. They see the ability to network as a means of succeeding in accomplishing their leadership tasks and goals. Some of them have received feedback about their need to improve how they work with others, their ability to build and manage cross-functional teams, and their capacity to broaden their influence beyond the authority of their position, to mention a few examples. To help leaders at all levels and in all kinds of organizations answer those kinds of challenges, CCL faculty is increasingly making its tacit understanding of the ties between networking and effective leadership more explicit. This book is one example of that effort.

Several streams of CCL research also support this approach to developing leadership networking skills. In essence, the ability to build, maintain, and use a network of people and resources reflects a capability associated with several essential leadership competencies, including resourcefulness, building and mending relationships, doing whatever it takes, and employing a participative management style. CCL's research shows that these four competencies are likely to remain important to the development of leaders' talent and the practice of leadership.

Key Point Summary

Leadership networking is not about collecting business cards or schmoozing. It's about building relationships and making alliances in service of others and in service of your organization's work and goals. A robust leadership network provides access to people, information, and resources.

Leadership networking demands authenticity. It trades in resources. It calls for a thoughtful and deliberate use of the power gained from your reputation, your alliances, and your position. Leadership networking requires skillful communication, negotiation, and conflict management.

In the process of building and maintaining relationships, you are likely to face a number of barriers, such as operational differences, level differences, demographic differences, and personal preferences. Other barriers include a lack of understanding of the big picture that your organization is working toward, time, location, previous relationship history, and change. Any one barrier can pose a challenge to effective networking; often a number of factors conspire to prevent good networks from developing.

In order to assess your network, think about your current priorities or leadership challenges. Create a network diagram directly related to your key challenge. Rank the people in your diagram in terms of their importance to you in facing your challenge, and in this way identify your most important relationships. Then diagnose any weaknesses and gaps in your network. Reflect and clarify your situation prior to setting networking goals.

Once you understand how your present network is structured, who is involved, and where you can push your network to the next level, you can take action using these eight strategies: learning from others, inviting others, inviting yourself, asking for feedback, working with others, being direct, being an information hub, and making allies.

Many of the roles and skills expected and required of leaders today are connected to networking. By seeing networking as an integral part of your role as a leader and by taking action to develop and nurture related skills, you begin to create benefits for yourself, your group, and your organization.

Ordering Information

TO GET MORE INFORMATION, TO ORDER OTHER IDEAS INTO ACTION GUIDEBOOKS, OR TO FIND OUT ABOUT BULK-ORDER DISCOUNTS, PLEASE CONTACT US BY PHONE AT 336-545-2810 OR VISIT OUR ONLINE BOOKSTORE AT WWW.CCL.ORG/ GUIDEBOOKS.

CPSIA information can be obtained
at www.ICGtesting.com
Printed in the USA
BVHW061948180121
598091BV00007B/41